Original title:

Branches of Joy and Wonder

Author: Dorian Ashford

ISBN HARDBACK: 978-9916-94-374-8

ISBN PAPERBACK: 978-9916-94-375-5

Unraveling the Knot of Serene Wonders

In a garden of giggles, I planted a smile,
Sunflowers danced, each with its own style.
Bees wore tiny hats, buzzing in tune,
While daisies played chess under the moon.

A squirrel told jokes, his tail in a twist,
Acorns went flying, could not be missed!
Trees chuckled softly, tickled by breeze,
As clouds shaped like elephants floated with ease.

Rainbows in socks, prancing with flair,
Puddles like mirrors, reflecting the air.
The wind played the flute, or was it a broom?
While flowers shared stories, all bright in bloom.

Then came a frog, crowned with a hat,
He croaked a delight, what's funnier than that?
With laughter unspooled and joy bubbling high,
This world spun in circles beneath a pink sky.

The Garden of Merriment

In a patch where giggles grow,
Flowers dance, swaying slow.
Bunnies hop with silly glee,
Tickling toes with sprightly spree.

Butterflies wear hats so bright,
Joking with the sun's warm light.
Bees hum tunes that tickle ears,
Filling every heart with cheers.

Winds whisper secrets of delight,
Making clouds look just polite.
Snails slide by in casual style,
While laughter lingers for a while.

A jester frog on lily pads,
Freestyle leaps, no room for fads.
In this place where fun is king,
Every leaf is a playful thing.

Laughter's Serenade in Bloom

A tulip with a crooked grin,
Sways its head as breezes spin.
Dandelions puff like cream,
Sharing smiles, a sweet daydream.

Laughter echoes through the air,
Bouncing off the flowers fair.
Petals flutter, hats in tow,
Breezy jokes begin to flow.

Jolly ants on picnic grounds,
March in rhythm, making sounds.
Crickets join the raucous band,
Creating tunes across the land.

Here, silliness reigns supreme,
Nature weaves a cheerful theme.
With every bloom, a hearty cheer,
In this serenade of joy, sincere.

Sun-kissed Moments of Bliss

Sunbeams tickle all the leaves,
Chasing shadows, oh good grief!
Caterpillars throw confetti,
As laughs bounce, light and petty.

The daisies wear their shades of blue,
Strutting like a joyful crew.
Squirrels joke with passing birds,
Trading winks instead of words.

A tiny mouse in slippers red,
Dances on a flower bed.
Winks at bees on buzzing spree,
Creating sweet symphonies.

Sun-kissed laughter fills the air,
Every whimsy laid quite bare.
In these moments, life's a jest,
Where fun and frolic never rest.

The Infinity of Opalescent Joy

In a world where giggles spark,
Clouds play tag, lighting the dark.
Raindrops laugh as they do fall,
Watering dreams for one and all.

Colors burst with playful cheer,
Each hue sings, "Come play, my dear!"
Grasshoppers hop in polka dots,
They've planned a dance to tie all knots.

With every twist, the joy expands,
Dancing wildly in vibrant bands.
The sun can't help but join the play,
Throwing rays in a merry array.

Infinite are the laughs we share,
In this place without a care.
Moments bounce like bubbles bright,
A symphony of pure delight.

Stories Woven in Green Trails

In the forest, squirrels play,
Hiding nuts, come what may.
One wears a tiny hat,
While another chases a cat.

Frogs with crowns sing at night,
While fireflies dance in delight.
The trees listen to their tales,
As the wind giggles and sails.

A turtle wearing shades strolls by,
Smiling gently at the sky.
He stops to greet a passing bee,
"Oh, what a busy life, you see!"

With every twist and turn, we find,
A world of laughter, beautifully blind.
These green trails whisper and tease,
Joy blooms in the rustling leaves.

Revelry Among the Twinkling Stars

The moon wears shades, looking cool,
While comets glide, they rule the pool.
Stars in gowns, twirl and sway,
Chasing meteors in a ballet.

A bear invites a cat to dance,
The owl shouts, "Give it a chance!"
They slide on clouds, a fluffy ride,
Shooting stars join the joyous tide.

Jupiter plays the tambourine,
While Saturn rolls in with a sheen.
Neptune cracks jokes that make us giggle,
And Mars moonwalks, oh what a wiggle!

Galaxies swirl with crazy cheer,
As aliens munch on space frontier.
In this night of cosmic fun,
Every heartbeat's a starry pun!

The Heart's Chorus in Bloom

In a garden, bees play chess,
While flowers bloom in fancy dress.
Roses giggle with their thorns,
As daisies toss around worn horns.

Tulips whisper, "What a day!"
As butterflies flutter and sway.
The daffodils break into song,
Humming loud what feels like wrong.

A hedgehog joins with funky beats,
While worms dance in wriggly feats.
The sun winks, playing hide and seek,
While the daisies cheer, "This is our peak!"

In every patch, a story's told,
Amid laughter, both young and old.
In this bloom of silly cheer,
The heart's bright chorus draws us near.

Harmony of Nature's Exuberance

The rocks roll 'round in playful jest,
While streams hum tunes of nature's best.
Crickets tap dance on the leaves,
As the wind teases through the eves.

Nutty squirrels throw acorn balls,
While trees echo the laughter's calls.
A chipmunk juggles as he hops,
While other woodland critters stop.

The sun peeks through with a grin,
Painting shadows on feral skin.
A parrot sports a top hat too,
Compliments from the skies, woohoo!

In every nook, the humor blooms,
Amidst the petals, nature looms.
This merry dance in vibrant hues,
Is life's sweet tune, one can't refuse.

Lifting Spirits Beyond the Leaves

In the park, a squirrel talks,
To the pigeons, mocks their walks.
The sun winks from up so high,
While a dog sneezes, oh my, oh my!

Laughter echoes, kids do play,
As a cat joins in the fray.
Chasing shadows, what a sight,
As ice cream drips, oh what a bite!

Balloons dance, caught in flight,
Chasing dreams, morning to night.
A bird with socks, oh what a tease,
It hops and flops with perfect ease.

Leaves ripple in the gentle breeze,
Tickling noses, teasing knees.
Joy spills out, a funny sound,
Like ticklish hugs all around!

Canvas of Hidden Smiles

Under the sun, kids with paint,
Splashing colors, oh what a saint!
A dog rolls in yellow, quite the thrill,
With giggles and laughter that never still.

A cat peeks out from a box so small,
Pretending to be a monsoon squall.
While birdies chirp like music notes,
Sailing in skies on butterfly boats.

A brush in hand, they make a mess,
But in their hearts, joy's no less.
An airplane shaped from paper flies,
As giggles burst, it almost cries!

Clouds like cotton candy swirl,
Tickled by winds, they giggle and twirl.
Each stroke a chuckle, oh what style,
In this canvas, we paint a smile!

A Tapestry of Bright Horizons

A pirate hat atop my head,
Ran past the fence, the dog was fed.
With treasure maps drawn on my palm,
The world's a stage, and life's a psalm!

With a wink, the sun shines bright,
As ants march on in pure delight.
Searching for sweets, on a quest,
Who knew an adventure could be this blessed?

Kites tug at strings, soar and dive,
While laughter bubbles, let's come alive!
The clouds play hide and seek today,
As friends join in, hip-hip-hooray!

Magic sprinkles in the air,
As butterflies dance without a care.
This tapestry we weave with cheer,
Bright horizons beckon, always near!

Joyful Notes in the Wind's Embrace

The wind hums through the trees like a song,
Tickling leaves, where laughter belongs.
A gnome with boots that squeak so loud,
Struts through the park, feeling so proud.

Chasing lost hats, a prank unfolds,
As the wind spins tales, wildly bold.
A kite gets caught in a ticklish dance,
Twisting and turning, oh what a chance!

With each gust, giggles take flight,
As children discover pure delight.
A frog croaks jokes, chubby and round,
In this garden, silly joy is found.

As bubbles float up high and free,
The world spins bright with easy glee.
In the wind's embrace, we find our tune,
Dancing together, morning to moon!

Whispers of a Sunlit Grove

In a grove where giggles play,
The squirrels dance in bright ballet,
The sunbeams tickle, shadows prance,
While rabbits join the silly dance.

A breeze tells jokes with rustling leaves,
As bumblebees wear tiny weaves,
The mushrooms chuckle, round and stout,
While daisies whisper, 'Look, no doubt!'

The grasshopper croons a sunny tune,
As clouds burst forth with laughter soon,
The trees sway gently, what a sight,
And fireflies twinkle in delight.

Let's celebrate the whimsy here,
With nature's joy that brings good cheer,
In a sunlit grove where glee takes flight,
We dance with shadows till the night.

Echoes of Laughter Beneath the Canopy

Beneath the leaves where sunbeams weave,
The chatter of a squirrel's heave,
Echoes of laughter all around,
In this silly, leafy playground.

A woodpecker's drumming, oh so keen,
Rhythms that rival any machine,
The turtles chuckle in their shell,
While crickets sing their raucous bell.

Jumpy frogs join in with their croaks,
Telling jokes that'll make you choke,
As butterflies wear hats so bright,
They giggle at the sheer delight.

In this lively space of joy and whim,
Nature pulls off her happy hymn,
So join the fun, don't miss a beat,
With echoes dancing at your feet.

Petals of Merriment

A daisy smiled at me today,
'Why so gloomy? Come, let's play!'
With petals shining all around,
Joy in colors can be found.

The roses winked, a cheeky tease,
While violets swayed in the gentle breeze,
The sunflowers struck a pose so grand,
Waving hello to every hand.

The tulips gathered for a chat,
In silly hats and chatting pat,
While poppies painted the meadow bright,
They laughed and twirled in pure delight.

With nature's giggles filling the air,
Every bloom has a tale to share,
Come share a laugh with petals near,
Where merriment blooms year after year.

The Dance of Dappled Light

In the woodland, light skips and hops,
Like a jester with funny tops,
Dancing shadows play hide and seek,
While cozy creatures laugh and peek.

The sunbeams twist in playful glee,
While overgrown thickets converse with the bee,
As mushrooms throw a little bash,
Their party hats all hedgehogs smash!

The hedges hum a melody sweet,
While ants march on with tiny feet,
The sunlight sparkles on the stream,
As frogs croak loudly, causing a scream.

Join the dance in this fairy tale,
Where laughter echoes without fail,
In dappled light, in joyful sight,
We spin and twirl till the fall of night.

Chasing Shadows of Happiness

In the park, we run so fast,
Tripping over shadows cast,
Laughter echoes, what a sight,
As squirrels join our silly flight.

With ice cream melting down our hands,
We're pirates sailing rubber bands,
Chasing giggles, oh what fun,
Underneath the blazing sun!

The grass tickles our bare toes,
As we dodge those funny crows,
With antics, we laugh till we cry,
Who knew happiness could fly?

In our hearts, this joy ignites,
As we chase our playful sights,
Forever young, in dreams we roam,
In the laughter, we find our home.

Ribbons of Light Through the Forest

We wander through the leafy maze,
Where sunlight dances in a haze,
Nature whispers jokes and puns,
While shadows play like silly nuns.

A squirrel juggles acorns there,
We pause to watch without a care,
The sunlight trickles, oh so bright,
Like ribbons weaving pure delight.

We spot a toad in a top hat,
With a bow and a sprightly spat,
His dance is quirky, oh so grand,
As we clap and form a band!

With every step, our giggles grow,
In this forest of radiant glow,
The laughter rolls like gentle streams,
In every rustling leaf, it seems.

Memories Carried by the Breeze

A breeze that tickles my silly hair,
Brings memories of a funny bear,
He wore a tutu, danced with flair,
And made us all stop and stare.

We chase the clouds, with faces bright,
Inventing stories, what a sight,
Kites become dragons in the air,
Our laughter floats without a care.

Each gust that passes, brings a cheer,
Of jumping frogs and frolicking deer,
While whispers of joy swirl around,
In the breeze, pure fun is found.

As we stand and marvel near,
Every giggle grows sincere,
With the breeze, we can't resist,
A memory we can't quite miss.

The Language of Blossoming Joy

In the garden, flowers chatter loud,
With secrets shared among the crowd,
Petals giggle, bees take flight,
As we dance among the light.

The daisies wink, the roses sway,
Making friends in their own way,
With butterfly jokes, they take a chance,
Encouraging us to laugh and dance.

A cactus grins from the dry land,
While daisies offer a helping hand,
In every bloom, a funny tale,
Of skunks that try to hide their smell.

We weave through colors, joy in bloom,
Creating laughter that fills the room,
In this garden, we can't stay shy,
For laughter's the language, oh my, oh my!

Tender Threads of Exhilaration

In the garden, squirrels dance,
They wear tiny pants, what a chance!
Bouncing high with acorns in tow,
Who knew that nuts could make them glow?

Bubbles float like dreams in the breeze,
Tickling leaves and buzzing bees.
A cat in shades naps with flair,
Dreaming of catching a flying hare.

Wobbling turtles race a snail,
Creating laughs on their silly trail.
A crow takes notes, he's quite the bard,
Singing rhymes in the backyard.

With giggles bright as sunlit streams,
Life's a circus bursting at the seams.
So let's twirl, spin, and hop around,
In this joy-filled, quirky playground!

The Dappled Path to Euphoria

A frog on a lily pad sings loud,
Typically shy but feeling proud.
He throws a party for all his pals,
Balloons and snacks for the little owls.

Butterflies wear party hats galore,
While ants deliver snacks to the floor.
They're having fun without a care,
With a sprinkle of magic in the air.

Now a grasshopper joins the tune,
Playing hopscotch beneath the moon.
His leg-shaking moves catch all the eyes,
As fireflies twinkle in the night skies.

Laughter echoes, as stars gleam bright,
In this dappled wonder, pure delight.
So come, let's skip down this wild trail,
Where silliness and glee shall prevail!

Blossoming Inspirations

Sunflowers wear glasses, very chic,
Sporting styles that seem quite unique.
They gossip about the cacti next door,
Who complain of the sun and just want more.

A dandy bee buzzes with glee,
Stealing honey while sipping tea.
With a monocle perched on his eye,
He swears he'll win the grand prize pie.

The daffodils giggle, heads held high,
Competing in hats made from the sky.
Their petals bright in a fashion show,
Challenging clouds to join the frolic below.

Dandelions whisper wild dreams,
With wishes riding on soft moonbeams.
In this floral feast of whimsical cheers,
We find delight throughout the years!

Streams of Ecstatic Whispers

Down by the brook, they gather in line,
The fish wear ties, looking so fine.
They splash about with joyful spins,
While turtles cheer for their corkscrew fins.

A raccoon in boots plays a flute,
Jamming tunes that are rather cute.
The toads croak in a hapless beat,
Marching along on their webbed little feet.

The willows wave, sharing their grace,
With a dance-off that sets the pace.
A squirrel judges with a tiny score,
Each twirl and leap leaves them wanting more.

As twilight wraps the day in a bow,
The laughter flows, like water's flow.
In these streams where happiness flows,
Whispers of joy are all that one knows!

Glimmers of Tranquility's Touch

In a world of silly socks,
The flip-flops dance and prance,
A cat on a skateboard,
Can't help but take a chance.

Balloons float like clouds,
And giggles burst like piñatas,
The coffee spills in laughter,
As sandwiches wear their hats.

Socks are mismatched today,
With stripes and dots in tow,
A juggling bear on skates,
Makes everyone go whoa!

Through the window, a parade,
Of squeaky toys and glee,
Where whimsy winds its way,
And joy is wild and free.

Shadows of Playful Surprises

Look! A shoe that squeaks,
And random llamas roam,
Underneath the rainbow,
They laugh by their own home.

Surprises hide in cupboards,
With prankster mice at play,
They wear tiny party hats,
And dance the night away.

Topsy-turvy giggles flow,
Like lemonade in spring,
Toasters pop with cheer,
And give the bread a fling.

So keep your eyes wide open,
In every nook and space,
You might just find a monkey,
With a very funny face.

Swaying to the Rhythm of Ecstasy

When the moon gets a jiggle,
And stars do a twirl,
The night sky starts to giggle,
As chaos starts to whirl.

A dance-off with a toaster,
That pops and spins around,
Toast flies in all directions,
What a booming sound!

Bubbles bounce like bunnies,
With happiness in tow,
Silly hats and wiggly feet,
Make the whole world glow.

So grab your favorite partner,
And dive into the fun,
Let laughter be the music,
Until the day is done.

The Fragrance of Infinitesimal Joy

In a garden full of giggles,
Grow cupcakes on a tree,
The scent of sweet confusion,
Is the best, you'll agree.

Ladybugs wear sunglasses,
As they sip on lemonade,
And ants play hide-and-seek,
Underneath the shade.

Sunflowers are the trumpets,
That yell with all their might,
While daisies twirl in circles,
Welcome the sunshine bright.

So skip along the pathways,
With laughter as your guide,
You'll find the joy of moments,
Just waiting for the ride.

Echoes of Lightheartedness

A squirrel in a suit sings a tune,
Dancing 'neath the bright afternoon sun.
With a hat made of cheese, he's quite a sight,
Chasing shadows, oh what a light!

In the park, a dog wears cool shades,
While a cat plays the drums in odd parades.
The flowers giggle as they sway,
With petals that laugh and skip away.

A snail tells tales of his wild dreams,
Of racing yachts and chocolate streams.
And in the breeze, a kite takes flight,
Waving 'Hello!' with all of its might.

Laughter spills like lemonade, sweet,
Shoes with wheels take off on little feet.
In this world, fun seems to bloom,
As we dance in the garden of a sunny room.

Ferns of Fantasy and Cheer

A frog in a tux jumps to the beat,
While polka-dot mushrooms tap their feet.
With every hop, he steals the show,
In this whimsical world where giggles grow.

The daisies wear hats, each one a flair,
Dancing in circles without a care.
A butterfly joins, with a wink and a glide,
On a petal parade, they all take pride.

A rainbow fish tells jokes from the creek,
As the bunnies chuckle, their laughter unique.
The stars above twinkle with glee,
In this land of shadows, joy is free.

With magic bursts in the evening glow,
We twirl and whirl, putting on quite a show.
With each silly dance, the laughter's wide,
In a garden of giggles, we all collide.

The Spiritual Leaves of Exuberance

A parrot recites phrases it knows,
Cracking jokes while striking a pose.
The trees elate as they sway in tune,
While the moon chuckles, a cheeky cartoon.

In the meadow, a goat wears a crown,
While a hedgehog spins, never to frown.
With each little laugh, the flowers bloom bright,
Creating a scene that's a pure delight.

Toadstools giggle, tickled by rain,
While a wise old owl winks with no strain.
The wind whispers secrets as it plays,
In a world where whimsy fills all the days.

Sunbeams bounce with a skip and a hop,
Making shadows dance, never to stop.
In a forest of chuckles, the spirits rise,
With smiles so bright, they light up the skies.

The Glow of Hidden Treasures

A treasure map drawn on a napkin case,
Leads to giggles at a funny place.
Where apples wear spectacles, quite bizarre,
And candy canes push their tiny car.

The old oak tree holds secrets untold,
While squirrels enact a play, bold and old.
Pine cones for crowns in their playful fest,
In this land of joy, they'll never rest.

The sunbeams dance with a silly wig,
A lighthearted puppet doing a jig.
In the glow of the lanterns that shimmer and sway,
Even shadows join in, having their play.

And when the stars twinkle down with cheer,
The laughter echoes, bright and clear.
In this quirky haven where smiles measure,
Life's simple moments are true hidden treasures.

Beneath the Canopy of Dreams

Under leaves so bright and green,
Squirrels dance, a comical scene.
With acorns flying through the air,
It's a nutty show, beyond compare.

Monkeys swing from vine to vine,
Sharing jokes, oh so divine.
While birds chirp in a silly tune,
They mock the sun, a bright balloon.

Giggling bees buzz all around,
Tickling flowers without a sound.
While shadows play, and laughter swells,
A whimsical dance in nature dwells.

In this realm where laughter reigns,
Even clouds wear happy strains.
Oh, to frolic, to laugh, to play,
Beneath the sky, let's seize the day!

Blossoms of Serendipity

In a garden where mishaps bloom,
A chicken sings to a hungry groom.
While flowers giggle in the sun,
They hide from bunnies on the run.

Rabbits wear hats, a sight to see,
Dancing to tunes from a nearby tree.
With daisies winking, oh so sly,
They toss their petals up to the sky.

A ladybug slips on dew-drenched grass,
As butterflies giggle and pass.
In this patch of pure delight,
Every moment feels just right.

With each bloom a cheer, a jest,
Nature laughs, oh what a fest!
In this land of silly whim,
Joy leaps high, as moments brim.

Unfolding Petals of Delight

Petals twirl on whimsy's breeze,
While grasshoppers hop with ease.
Their dance is quite the silly sight,
In the glow of morning light.

A bumblebee attempts to sing,
But stumbles on his tiny wing.
Flowers blush with giggling faces,
As honey drips from charming places.

The daisies exchange glances sly,
As butterflies flutter and fly.
With every laugh, a sparkle grows,
In this garden where fun flows.

As petals fold, a secret pact,
To make each moment a fun act.
Joy blooms bright in every hue,
In this realm of antics new.

The Symphony of Lively Spirits

Beneath the shade where shadows play,
A frog croaks tunes to start the day.
While crickets strum their tiny strings,
The air is filled with laughter's wings.

A parade of ants all march in sync,
With hats made of leaves — what do you think?
Silly squirrels steal the show,
Rolling acorns, a joyful throw.

The sun shines brightly on this spree,
As petals twist in jubilee.
Amidst the fun and games they share,
Every heartbeat sings without a care.

Oh, what a riot! Oh, what a sound!
In this melody, joy abounds.
Nature's orchestra plays its part,
Creating laughter that warms the heart.

A Tapestry of Blissful Moments

In a world where socks go missing,
Mismatched pairs hold a certain charm.
Laughter spills when we start kissing,
Breezes lift our spirits, warm.

A tumble here, a pancake flip,
Butterflies dance in our tummies.
Cupcakes bounce on a sugar trip,
Oh, the joy, it surely hums.

Kite strings tangling in our hair,
Silly hats worn with great pride.
Rainbow sprinkles everywhere,
In this trip, we're all the guide.

With each giggle, the world spins bright,
A treasure trove of playful blunders.
Chasing rainbows, pure delight,
Life's silly twists are the best wonders.

Celestial Rays of Happiness

Under the sun, we slide and glide,
Worms wear shades, so hip and cool.
Squirrels dance with a furry pride,
While we shout, 'Let's break the rule!'

Galaxies twirl in cosmic games,
Stars wink like eyes at our silly show.
Float like marshmallows, without names,
Sprinkling joy wherever we go.

Woodpeckers drum to our playful tune,
Chasing bubbles that float and drift.
Even the moon can't help but swoon,
As we craft laughter—a splendid gift.

In haystack forts, we claim our throne,
Puppies tumble, all feet and frolic.
A circus of joy, no need for a bone,
With giggles and hearts, life's so iconic.

The Garden of Infinite Possibilities

In the garden where daisies tease,
A frog sings opera with grandeur flair.
Bushes tickle the buzzing bees,
Each petal a giggle draped in air.

Rabbits hop, wearing silly shoes,
Grapes roll down like laughter's sound.
Sunlight sprinkles, the colors fuse,
In this patch, fun knows no bound.

Caterpillars doing the cha-cha,
While ladybugs twirl in delight.
Even the weeds know how to salsa,
As nature dances in sheer light!

With every bloom, there's laughter arrange,
Butterflies drift on whimsical flights.
In this place, every moment's strange,
Creating joy, amidst day and night.

Colorful Threads of Enchantment

In a world stitched with giggles and glue,
Tangled yarn, it pulls at our seams.
Odd socks chatter in colors so true,
Woven tales sprout from our dreams.

The merry-go-round spins with a song,
Cats and dogs sing in perfect sync.
Fuzzy hats and glasses go along,
In this crazy world, we never blink.

Pudding fights break out with delight,
While our laughter echoes through the air.
With a wink and a spin, hearts take flight,
The magic resides in this funny affair.

So join the quilt of joy we create,
Each moment a thread, vibrant and fun.
In this tapestry, we celebrate,
The beauty of life, together as one.

Celebrating Life Under a Verdant Ceiling

In the shade of great green leaves,
We laugh as the gentle breeze weaves.
Squirrels perform their acrobatic stunts,
While we cheer for their daring fronts.

Picnics ruled by ants and crumbs,
They march like tiny, hungry drums.
Each sandwich a royal invitation,
To nature's grand celebration.

Sunlight dances, flickering free,
On this spectacle, don't you agree?
With friends and laughter, here we find,
A joyful chaos, richly designed.

Life blooms in the most whimsical ways,
In this joyful theater, our hearts play.
Under the canopy, we plot and scheme,
To revel in this silly, bright dream.

The Art of Delight in Nature's Realm.

In a meadow where daisies chime,
The butterflies groove, oh so sublime.
With each flutter, they giggle and tease,
Turning petals into joyous knees.

A rabbit hops, with hat in tow,
Claiming he's off to steal the show!
While turtles in shades plot their next race,
Thinking slow is the best way to face.

Trees tell stories through windswept cheer,
As blueberries burst—oh, what a year!
We toast with lemonade, laughter our drink,
In gardens of whimsy, we pause and think.

Birds gather round, to witness the fun,
As we dance in circles, two by one.
Nature's palette paints with a wink,
In this festival, we happily sink.

Whispers of Radiance

A bird on a branch sings notes of glee,
While squirrels plot mischief under the tree.
With acorns as hats, they invite us to play,
In this curious world, come join the ballet!

Butterflies prance, with colors so bold,
Dancing on flowers, their stories unfold.
A picnic of laughter spills onto the ground,
As nature's own laughter is sweetly unbound.

The sun throws confetti, a golden embrace,
While shadows shimmy, they know how to grace.
In whispers of breezes, giggles are caught,
In this peaceful haven, happiness is sought.

Every rustle and chirp, a chorus of charm,
With nature composing its own joyful psalm.
In this tapestry of life, we unwind,
Discovering wonders, and laughter entwined.

The Dance of Laughter's Echo

In meadows where silly shadows play,
The daisies hold a raucous soirée.
With bees in bow ties, buzzing in style,
They sip on nectar and mingle awhile.

Jumping jays and owls with glasses askew,
Join in the dance as the sun bids adieu.
We twirl with delight, under twilight's gaze,
For every laugh's echo, in this joyful maze.

Crickets chirp, their legs a percussion,
While frogs leap in a grand introduction.
With each splash, laughter bounces from pond,
Making memories that last and respond.

As night blankets all in a starry embrace,
The moon chuckles softly, keeping the pace.
In this festive fluff of giggles and cheer,
We treasure each moment, holding them dear.

Harvesting Moments of Bliss

With laughter ripe, we shake the tree,
Plucking giggles, oh so free.
Every chuckle, a tasty treat,
A harvest danced on happy feet.

Silly shadows chase the sun,
Wobbly races, oh what fun!
Ticklish winds, a playful breeze,
Gently pulling at our knees.

Juggling dreams with eyes so wide,
In a circus where we glide.
Each moment, a balloon in flight,
Bouncing high in pure delight.

So let us gather, hand in hand,
Savoring joy, a merry band.
These moments, sweet, we'll not dismiss,
A feast of laughter, pure bliss.

Rhapsody Under the Stars

Under twinkling lights we sing,
A chorus made of everything.
Each star a wink, a cosmic prank,
In the night, our joy, we tank.

Shooting stars, like candy flies,
Whirling dreams that mesmerize.
With giggles shared, our hearts take flight,
In this rhapsody of the night.

Kites of laughter in the air,
Wobbly wishes without a care.
Moonbeams tickle our glowing skin,
In this dance, where fun begins.

Together we craft a silly song,
In this moment, nothing feels wrong.
With every note, a sparkle's chance,
Under the stars, we twirl and prance.

The Luminescent Maze of Interest

In the glow of silly signs,
We wander through the twisty lines.
Curiosity, our bright guide,
With every turn, more laughs reside.

Bouncing through this maze of glee,
Finding treasures, you and me.
Jokes and giggles hide away,
In every corner where we play.

Luminous paths of quirky sights,
Glowing dreams and goofy lights.
Each step brings a happy surprise,
In this maze, we realize.

We're explorers on this quest,
Where whimsy puts our joy to test.
With every twist and turn we greet,
Life's a maze, oh so sweet.

Beckoning to the Realm of Delight

With candy canes and fuzzy hats,
We invite you here—come, sit with cats!
In a realm where all's absurd,
Every chuckle's simply stirred.

Cupcakes dance across the floor,
While jolly giggles beg for more.
Ticklish tales that never cease,
Painting joy, our heart's release.

Whirlwinds toss our doubts away,
In this corner where we play.
We leap and twirl, a dizzy flight,
Beckoning joy, with sheer delight.

So grab a friend, don't stay behind,
In this wonderland, we'll unwind.
Laughter echoes, sweet and bright,
Welcome to our realm of light.

Vibrant Trails of Serendipity

Skip along the winding path,
Chasing giggles, feeling daft.
With every turn, a surprise awaits,
A dancing squirrel, a feast of plates.

Sunlight winks from leafy spots,
A pickle jar holds all the thoughts.
Riding bikes with squeaky brakes,
Muffin crumbs and silly flakes.

Rusty swings make a creaky sound,
As we leap high above the ground.
Hiccups bloom like dandelion seeds,
Twirling joy as laughter feeds.

Let's paint the sky in rainbow hues,
With laughter splashed like morning blues.
Each step taken is a giggly game,
In this whimsical and zany frame.

Swaying with Laughter

Underneath the wobbly tree,
Silly monkeys swing carefree.
They tell us jokes that make us snort,
While sipping juice from a paper quart.

Ticklish grass beneath our toes,
The wind plays tag as laughter flows.
With ice cream dripping down our chins,
We dance around, like goofy twins.

Clouds roll by with fluffy thrills,
Bouncing balls and laughter spills.
A puppy joins with muddy paws,
Swaying gleefully without a cause.

In this realm where giggles reign,
All our worries seem so plain.
Let's twirl and skip until we fall,
In a world where fun's the call.

The Elixir of Morning Dew

As dawn breaks with frosty cheer,
We sip the dew, our hearts sincere.
Giggling ghosts of yesterday,
Why does syrup have its way?

Jelly beans sprout from the ground,
With every bite, pure joy is found.
The sun sneezes, and we erupt,
With fits of laughter, joy abrupt.

Frogs in ties give business tips,
While ants perform their tiny flips.
Licorice vines entwined in knots,
A path of fun that never trots.

This morning brew is made for play,
With a sprinkle of whimsy, come what may.
May every giggle rise anew,
In a cup of magic, bold and true.

Skylark's Serenade

Up above, a skylark sings,
While the garden dances with springs.
Its tune tickles the sunny rays,
Bringing smiles in the funny ways.

Mice in boots throw a parade,
Stepping to a jig, unafraid.
They wave their hats and do a spin,
In this merry, cheerful din.

Feathered friends perform a show,
Waltzing with petals from below.
Each note a giggle floating high,
As butterflies join in the sky.

So let's sway with nature's tune,
And twirl about beneath the moon.
In this lively serenade we find,
Laughter echoes, sweet and kind.

The Wondrous Tangle of Life

A squirrel in a top hat, what a sight,
He juggles acorns, quite the delight!
The garden gnomes dance with flair,
While frogs in tuxedos sing in the air.

The grass tickles toes, laughter in play,
As clouds turn shapes, a giraffe on a tray.
Life's a circus, we're all the show,
Caught in the tangle, let the good times flow.

Butterflies sport ties, bees wear a grin,
In this topsy-turvy realm, let's dive in!
We'll chase the rainbows, splash in the sun,
And twist and twirl until we're done.

So tip your hat to the whimsical strife,
Embrace the quirks, it's the flavor of life!
Each tangled moment is a giggle or two,
So let's roam the world, just me and you.

Daydreams in Bloom

A daisy declares, 'I'm a queen of flair!'
With buttercups dancing, no worries, no care.
The sunflowers gossip about the day's news,
While tulips hold tea in their colorful shoes.

A bumblebee winks, pulling pranks in the breeze,
As daisies drop petals, not one, but a tease.
We giggle and wiggle, in this garden of cheer,
With flowers and laughter, there's nothing to fear.

The clouds play tag in a sky painted blue,
While rainbows sip lemonade and laugh too.
Let's skip on the petals, chase shadows that play,
In this blooming daydream, come join the ballet!

So gather your daisies and laugh as you go,
In this vibrant picnic, we'll steal the show!
Each moment's a flower, vibrant and bright,
Let's bloom with the joy, from morning to night.

The Enchanted Oasis of Delight

In a land where laughter flows like sweet tea,
Llamas in capes dance beneath the palm tree.
Coconuts sing in a chorus of cheer,
While turtles in sunglasses float near and dear.

The sand tickles toes in a tropical sight,
As iguanas recite poems of light.
We splash in the lagoon, mischief in our eyes,
With friendly flamingos teaching us to fly.

The sun dips down, painting skies with delight,
As crickets play music to dance through the night.
Let's twirl with the breezes, make wishes on stars,
In this place of enchantment, we'll conquer Mars!

So gather your giggles, your joy, and your fun,
This oasis of laughter has only begun!
With cocktails of bubbles, let's sway in the air,
In this magical haven, we have not a care.

Whimsy's Embrace

In a world where jellybeans grow on trees,
And marshmallow clouds float in the breeze.
A cat in a bowtie recites silly rhymes,
As pirates of giggles sail seas of good times.

The wind blows confetti, a colorful fight,
While pink elephants dance in the moonlight.
With spoons for our hats, we twirl in the park,
And cupcakes fly by, leaving trails of spark!

With laughter like bubbles that float on the air,
Dancing with shadows, not a worry, beware!
Each whimsy unfolding, a story untold,
In this quirky embrace, we spin out of control.

So let's skip through the daisies, our hearts in a race,
In this frolicsome world, find your happy place!
For giggles are treasures; they lighten our pace,
In this humor-filled tapestry, life's a sweet chase.

The Glade of Dreams Unfurled

In a glade where giggles sway,
Little frogs throw a party each day.
Twirling hats upon their heads,
Dancing leaves, jellybeans spread.

Squirrels join in a silly race,
Chasing tails with a furry grace.
Bluebirds chirp in a wild tune,
While the sun hummed a bright cartoon.

A mouse in shades, oh what a sight,
Disco balls reflect the light.
Fireflies buzz, showing their flair,
It's a fiesta—beyond compare!

The trees laugh and sway with cheer,
"No boring times, we're all right here!"
Nature's jesters, all in play,
Join the fun—hip hip hooray!

Echoes of Wonderment's Dance

Amidst the ferns, a rabbit pranced,
In boots too big, he looked entranced.
He slipped and slid, then sprang with glee,
A clumsy waltz, oh can't you see?

The owls chuckled in nearby trees,
While squirrels cracked nuts with the breeze.
They cheered him on with every fall,
"Come hop this way, let's have a ball!"

A tumble leaf joined in the fray,
Spinning 'round, it twirled away.
The scene was silly, a sight to find,
Nature's madness, one of a kind!

With echoes gleeful, the forest swayed,
Laughter wrapped the glade displayed.
Bunnies, bugs, and bear cubs too,
Joined the dance—come join us too!

Rainfall of Tender Smiles

A sprinkle here, a sprinkle there,
Raining smiles beyond compare.
The clouds wore hats, how absurdly grand,
Each drop a laugh, a ticklish hand.

Puddles giggled, rippling wide,
As ducks slid in, they did not hide.
"Take that, you" with a cheeky flap,
Splashing joy—what a funny trap!

The sun peeked out, all bright and bold,
Chasing rain with a warmth untold.
A rainbow arched with colors keen,
Said, "I bring glimmers, sweet and green!"

In this joyful weather spree,
All creatures danced so happily.
With every drop, a smile unfurled,
Happiness sprinkled across the world!

Seraphic Sounds of Elation

In a valley, notes began to prance,
Hummingbirds whipped up a merry dance.
Their wings a-flutter, a cheerful buzz,
A jubilant tune just because!

Daisies sang with a gentle sway,
While ants marched in a grand ballet.
Ticklish whispers and shouts of glee,
Filled the air, oh what a spree!

A bear played drums on a thumping log,
With a beat so sweet, it made clear the fog.
Every creature lent a helping hand,
Creating symphonies across the land!

The echoes lingered, soft and light,
Filling hearts with sheer delight.
With every note, the world mesmerized,
In this playful tune of joy, we all harmonized!

Mosaic of Delighted Hearts

Colors splash on canvas bright,
Laughter echoes through the night.
Tickles dance in breezy air,
Joyful prances everywhere.

Each smile shines like stars above,
Chasing ducks, we fall in love.
A juggling act of silly glee,
Who knew life's a comedy?

Riding bikes on wobbly wheels,
Spilling ice cream, what a deal!
Kites that flip and swirl around,
Catch the giggles, what a sound!

In this mix of silly fun,
Every heartbeat weighs a ton.
With happiness, we skip along,
Life's a merry, joyful song.

Secrets in the Shade

Underneath the leafy growth,
Squirrels chatter, taking oath.
Who stole my cookie? Not the bird!
In this chatter, truth is blurred.

Shadows play a hide-and-seek,
Tickling toes, oh what a peek!
Laughter spills from hidden spots,
As friendly creatures weave their plots.

Hats appear and wrong-way shoes,
Ants march by with grand reviews.
What's that buzzing? Bumblebee!
Oh, it's just a joke, you see?

In the shade, the secrets blend,
Every giggle seems to mend.
Acorn cups for little teas,
Life's a game; oh, what a breeze!

Pathways of Radiant Dreams

Bouncing balls and skipping stones,
Even cats are making bones!
Dancing shadows on the ground,
Where's the lost and found, we found!

Wizards wear their wands with flair,
While unicorns just chill and stare.
Leapfrog to the moonlit play,
Every moment brightens day.

Cloud divas drift in velvet skies,
They flip and twirl with happy sighs.
Wishful thoughts are spun like lace,
Chasing dreams, we find our place.

With wild giggles, joy takes flight,
Every corner glows with light.
Together in this vibrant scheme,
Life becomes our wildest dream.

Symphony of Sprightly Breezes

Winds that tickle through the trees,
Make the flowers dance with ease.
A melody of joyous cheer,
Listen close, the tunes are here.

Frogs in chorus croak their song,
While butterflies flit all day long.
Twirling fairies in the air,
Sprightly breezes everywhere!

Skip along and chase the light,
Socks mismatched, what a sight!
In this symphony of fun,
Every giggle weighs a ton.

Let's collect the sounds of glee,
Harmony, just you and me.
A cheeky wink, a bouncing leap,
Together in this joy, we keep.

The Orchard of Hope and Dreams

In an orchard filled with chatter,
Squirrels dance, a nutty patter.
Birds wear hats, a fashion spree,
While apples giggle from the tree.

Beneath the sun, a pig that twirls,
In his tutu, spinning swirls.
Fruits argue over who's more sweet,
A bickering feast, a silly treat.

Chickens play hopscotch on the grass,
In this world where giggles pass.
Bumblebees wear shades so cool,
Pollinating, the sassy fool.

Dreams hang ripe on branches high,
Underneath, the laughter's nigh.
Pick a joke, or maybe two,
In this orchard, joy's the view.

Sunshine Through Emerald Leaves

Under leaves of emerald hue,
Sunshine cracks jokes, just for you.
A butterfly slips on a slide,
With giggles echoing worldwide.

A squirrel sings an opera stout,
While the sun shines roundabout.
With shadows dancing on the floor,
Here, every step's a comedic score.

The raindrops cheer with tiny claps,
As frogs perform their little naps.
And in this circus made of light,
Even the sun fumbles with delight.

Each ray a wink, a playful tease,
Nature chuckles in the breeze.
Through emerald leaves, we'll always find,
A comedy show, pure and kind.

The Cascade of Laughter's Leaves

In a cascade where chuckles flow,
Leaves giggle, putting on a show.
A juggling rabbit by the brook,
While frogs read tales from a book.

Wobbly roots start to disco dance,
In the shade, the critters prance.
A tree frog splits a witty pun,
While creepy crawlies join the fun.

Laughter tumbles like a stream,
In this forest, dreams gleam.
An acorn tries to run away,
But nature laughs, and there it stays.

With every rustle, jokes emerge,
In a symphony, the giggles surge.
Nature's a stage, wild and free,
A comedy act for you and me.

Silken Threads of Joyful Existence

In the garden of woven threads,
Where every flower shares its spreads.
A spider weaves its tangling tales,
While laughter flirts with summer gales.

Bees hold meetings, wearing hats,
Discussing life with clever chats.
While daisies play hide and seek,
Their petal jokes are far from weak.

The sun tickles the tulips pink,
As ladybugs compose a wink.
Silken threads of giggles spun,
In this realm, there's so much fun.

Every bloom a punchline's gift,
In this world where spirits lift.
With every breeze, a laugh takes flight,
Joyful existence, pure delight.

Dancing Lights in the Canopy

In the trees, the lights do sway,
Like cheeky fireflies in a play.
They twinkle here, and wink on there,
A disco ball, without a care.

The squirrels groove with acorn hats,
While birds perform in feathered spats.
The branches shake, they twist and bend,
In this wild dance, there's no end.

A giggling breeze tickles the leaves,
As nature's sound machine believes.
They rustle tunes so light and free,
A whimsical cacophony!

And down below, we laugh and spin,
With woodland critters, we join in.
The canopy, a stage so grand,
In this bright world, we take a stand.

The Heart's Mosaic of Radiance

Colors burst from every side,
Like jellybeans that take a ride.
A patchwork quilt on nature's quilt,
With joy and laughter, the world is built.

A gingerbread house caught in a tree,
Where teddy bears sip honey tea.
The sun, a clown in painted hues,
With rainbow socks and polka dot shoes.

A whirl of petals in the breeze,
They tumble past like giggling bees.
They skip and hop, in pairs they prance,
Inviting all to join the dance.

With every hue and silly grin,
Life's grand mosaic will begin.
In laughter's echo, we will see,
The vibrant heart of harmony.

Curved Arches of Serenity

Beneath the bows of trees so grand,
Wobbly gnomes dance hand in hand.
With lazy smiles and funny hats,
They twirl around with giggling spats.

A yoga cat on a sunbeam's edge,
Teaches poses on a grassy ledge.
While frogs in crowns leap with intent,
To touch the clouds, they are hell-bent.

Each breezy whisper tells a tale,
Of mischievous winds that like to sail.
They tickle the leaves, and tease the air,
While clouds giggle and play peek-a-boo there.

In this arc of comfort, laughter reigns,
With wobbling worms on laughter's trains.
Beneath these arches, fun resides,
In nature's playground, joy abides.

A Canvas of Everlasting Joy

A canvas wide where colors splash,
Painted dreams in a joyful rash.
With flying paints and giggling brushes,
Creating scenes that make one blushes.

A laughing sun with a smile so wide,
Winking at clouds like a cheeky guide.
Each stroke of whimsy fills the day,
As laughter blooms in a bright bouquet.

The trees, they clap in vibrant cheer,
As melody cups the evening near.
With dancing puddles beneath our feet,
Each splash a note, oh what a treat!

In this grand art of joyful sights,
Where every heart takes playful flights.
We paint our stories bold and true,
On nature's canvas, me and you.

Dreams Riding the Rainbow

Up high above the ground, they zoom,
Laughter ties the colors, and they bloom.
A squirrel in a tutu, what a sight,
He leads the chase, oh what a flight!

With fluffy clouds as comfy chairs,
We munch on popcorn, free of cares.
A giraffe juggles fruits, quite the thrill,
While rainbows giggle, chasing the hill!

A pool of candy, deep and wide,
A bouncy castle, our joyful pride.
With every leap, we touch the stars,
As marshmallow mice drive candy cars!

At sunset's edge, we all conspire,
To roast our dreams over the fire.
So grab a friend and take a ride,
On this whimsical, wild joy tide!

The Spirit of Joy Takes Flight

A penguin skateboard zooms and slips,
Wearing sunglasses, doing tricks and flips.
With a belly flop, he steals the show,
As we cheer him on, in the glow!

Balancing on a rainbow's crest,
A squirrel struts, he's dressed the best.
With sparkly shoes, they stomp and prance,
While giggles float in a merry dance!

The clouds play tag, a fluffy chase,
With little stars that giggle and race.
A parade of wishes flits about,
On wings of dreams, let's scream and shout!

When sunlight tickles the grassy floor,
Ice cream showers rain from the sky's door.
So let's leap high, let worries flee,
In this quirky world, just you and me!

Enchanted Trails of Happiness

Through meadows of laughter, we run with glee,
Chasing the giggles, come join me!
A cat in a hat juggles cheese,
As daffodils dance in a gentle breeze!

Puppies in bow ties flip and bound,
As hummingbirds twirl round and round.
Each step whispers, 'What's your dream?'
While pixies chuckle and silver beams!

An owl with glasses reads the news,
While daisies hug and wear their shoes.
With every tickle from the sun's glow,
Happiness blooms where the wild things go!

So grab a wish, and hold it tight,
With playful hearts, let's take to flight.
We'll dance on clouds, roam fields of fun,
In this merry place, we've just begun!

Petals of Light in the Breeze

In a garden of giggles, where bright thoughts sprout,
We spin round and round, there's no doubt.
A frog in a bowler hat sings a tune,
As dancing flowers twirl under the moon!

Butterflies giggle, wearing balloons,
While bees on skateboards hum silly tunes.
Every petal whispers sweet delight,
In this dazzling dreamland, all feels right!

A ticklish breeze plays hide and seek,
With grass skipping, hideaways peek.
Every chuckle bounces through the air,
As pixies sprinkle laughter everywhere!

So let's gather wishes like shiny stones,
Sharing our shenanigans, joy overtones.
With glittering smiles, we celebrate,
In this whimsical realm where we create!

The Secret Grove of Light

In a grove where shadows dance,
The squirrels wear funny pants.
They leap and twirl in a silly way,
Chasing sunbeams through the day.

A rabbit near a rainbow beam,
Sips tea and dreams a wacky dream.
With hats made out of daffodil,
It's all quite bonkers, if you will!

The trees giggle in bright, green hues,
As birds crack jokes in fancy shoes.
A butterfly winks and flutters about,
In this joyful place, there's never doubt!

So skip along and join the fun,
Where every day feels like a pun.
The secret grove is full of cheer,
And laughter echoes far and near.

Harmonies in the Heart's Nook

In a nook where laughter sings,
The hedgehogs wear fuzzy rings.
They tap dance on a wooden floor,
While bumblebees hum folklore.

A parrot on a swing so high,
Cracks jokes that make the daisies sigh.
Flowers giggle with colors so bright,
In this nook, oh what delight!

The breeze tickles the leaves on trees,
As ladybugs sip minty teas.
They chatter loud with a cozy flair,
Creating melodies that fill the air.

So join the fun without a care,
In this happy, fragrant lair.
Where every moment brings sweet smiles,
And joy stretches for miles and miles!

Where Celestial Bodies Play

Under the stars, the comets glide,
With jokes that make the planets hide.
A moonbeam here, a star there,
In cosmic games, we leap and share.

The sun winks bright, but doesn't burn,
While dazzling orbits take a turn.
Galaxies giggle in twinkling light,
As they frolic through the endless night.

The asteroids tumble with silly glee,
Dancing around like they're carefree.
In every corner of the night sky,
You'll find mirth that'll make you sigh.

So join us in this cosmic spree,
Where laughter and stars are wild and free.
Embrace the joy, let your heart sway,
In the universe where we love to play!

A Journey Through Enchanted Canopies

Through the woods, a path unfolds,
Where mischief thrives and laughter molds.
Elves sip cocoa in cozy nooks,
While goblins read their funny books.

The tall trees chuckle as we pass by,
Whispering secrets with a sigh.
With branches swaying, making tunes,
Where light pokes through like merry moons.

A fox in boots rides a wheeled cart,
Delivering giggles with every start.
The mushrooms sprout with hats so bright,
In this whimsical world, pure delight!

So skip along this joyous quest,
Where every creature loves to jest.
With laughter blooming in every sunbeam,
This enchanted journey is a dream!

Streams of Enchanted Laughter

In a forest of giggles and glee,
Silly squirrels dance on the spree.
A rabbit in glasses reads a joke,
While trees do a twist, oh what a poke!

Bouncing clouds in the cotton-candy sky,
Tickle the leaves as they whistle by.
The frogs in bow ties croak out a tune,
As the moon starts to chuckle 'round noon!

With mushrooms in hats, the party is grand,
A parade of the odd, oh isn't it planned?
The fireflies giggle, their lights all a-spark,
As pencils take flight, doodling in the dark!

So chuckle along as the sun sets down,
In this merry old place, with its whimsical crown.
For laughter, dear friend, it sprinkles like dew,
In the streams of delight, it calls out to you!

Reflections in a Prism of Joy

A cat in a bow, with a mirror so bright,
Practices smiles in the soft morning light.
Bubbles burst forth as a dog trips and rolls,
And laughter erupts from the tickle of souls!

Raindrops in puddles play hop and skip,
While frogs on lily pads perfect their flip.
Each shimmer a dance, every sparkle a prank,
As the flowers wink, with an audible prank!

A hedgehog in shades hums a sweet little tune,
While paintings of giggles adorn the full moon.
The clouds wear their joy like a fluffy old coat,
As they sail on the breeze, on a laughter boat!

So gather, dear friends, with glee we embrace,
The wonders that tickle the heart in this place.
For in reflections, pure joy we have found,
A prism of laughter, spreading all 'round!

Seeds of Radiant Joy

In a garden where giggles sprout from the ground,
Seeds of delight cause the flowers to bound.
A butterfly giggles, then zooms in a whirl,
While the sun has a tickle-fight with a girl!

Each daisy a dancer with petals aglow,
Spinning in circles, puts on quite a show.
The breeze steals a grin from the leaves up above,
And whispers sweet secrets of laughter and love!

As pumpkins in tutus host waltzes at night,
They juggle the stars, what a marvelous sight!
The carrots wear crowns, in a festival air,
Where veggies and laughter are spun everywhere!

So plant all your dreams in this garden of glee,
Where seeds of delight blossom wild and free.
For in every corner, there's joy to implore,
A riot of laughter, forever in store!

Journeys Through the Sunlit Grove

In a grove where giggles burst forth with delight,
Silly shadows prance in the soft morning light.
With a bear in a cape, who can't find his chair,
And a turtle in sneakers that zoomed like a flare!

The path leads us on with a skip and a bounce,
Past trees that all twist, making laughter pronounce.
A fox in a top hat offers us pie,
While the owl spreads joy, still stirring the sky!

A dance of the stars, the moon brings a grin,
As the flowers perform their melodious spin.
From daisies to dandelions, joy fills the air,
As squirrels play tunes with the rabbits in pairs!

So follow the sounds through this magical place,
Where laughter and fun line the path we embrace.
For in every step, a chuckle will rise,
On this journey of wonder beneath friendly skies!

Mysteries Among the Green

In a garden, a cat in a hat,
Dances around like a chubby acrobat.
The daisies chuckle, the lilies wave,
Watching him twirl, oh how they behave!

A squirrel with glasses reads tales of old,
While butterflies giggle, gossip unfolds.
The sunbeams wink, passing a joke,
As frogs on the lily pads croak, 'You're broke!'

A snail in a race, steals glances with glee,
While ants rock the party with tea and a spree.
Each leaf a tale, each twig a dance,
In this quirky realm, behold the chance!

So come one and all, to sit by the trees,
Where laughter is sprouted, carried by breeze.
With whimsy and charm, and tickles galore,
In the green where the mysteries softly roar!

Kaleidoscope of Smiles

A giraffe in a tutu prances about,
With flamingo friends, there's no hint of doubt.
They twirl and they leap, oh what a sight!
While a squirrel DJ spins tracks day and night.

The daisies wear glasses, debating the rain,
While snails start a band, they're singing the same.
A cricket in costume recites silly poems,
As the breeze carries whispers from bright colored homes.

Butterflies laugh in a vibrant parade,
While a turtle's high-fiving, his fun never fades.
In this wild gallery of colors and cheer,
Each smile is a splash, painting dreams oh so clear!

So gather your friends, take a seat on the grass,
Join the giggles and wiggles, let no moment pass.
This kaleidoscope world invites you to play,
Bring on the laughter, hip-hip-hooray!

Harmonics of Unseen Wonders

In a meadow of mirth, where the oddities sing,
A sound-making chicken finds joy in the spring.
With a quack and a cluck, they form quite the tune,
Bouncing off daisies, beneath the bright moon.

A frog on a drum, keeping beat with a smile,
Waltzes with beetles, they go the extra mile.
Each note is a giggle, each rhythm a cheer,
As ants tap their feet, oh, let's draw them near!

Monkeys in capes, juggling socks on the fly,
Sharing ticklish secrets as clouds whisper by.
A symphony blooms in the grass and the air,
Gather all creatures, come share in this flair!

So tune in your hearts, let the chorus unfold,
In this field of enchantment, there's laughter untold.
Join the unseen wonders that dance in the light,
With harmonics of joy to sparkle the night!

The Illuminated Path to Whimsy

On a path made of candy, with gumdrops galore,
Where unicorns giggle and squirrels explore.
Lollipops whisper the sweetest of dreams,
As jellybeans bounce in their vibrant teams.

A parade of the quirky is sure to ensue,
With waffles and syrup, it calls out to you!
Clouds made of marshmallow float gently above,
As fireflies whisper—a message of love.

Now, a hedgehog plays hopscotch, no one takes heed,
While kites tied to kittens lift spirits like speed.
The sprightly green grass teases toes as they stroll,
With each giggle echoing, it's good for the soul!

So wander this path, let your heart take a leap,
Where whimsy and laughter wake hopes from their sleep.

In this illuminated garden, find wonders anew,
With joy on the wind, and a sprinkle of dew!

9 789916 943748